DAVID T. L

THREE SAMS

for Percussion Solo

HENDON MUSIC

BOOSEY & HAWKES

DISTRIBUTED BY

HAL•LEONARD®
7777 W. BLUEMOUND RD. P.O. BOX 13819 MILWAUKEE, WI 53213

www.boosey.com
www.halleonard.com

PROGRAM NOTE

Each of the *Three Sams* explores a different challenge.

In *(—)-I-Am*, a perpetual motion figure in the vibraphone is redistributed among the other instruments of the set-up. Melodic pitches are replaced with their closest non-pitched equivalent—i.e. the cowbell, sounding an approximate F replaces an F on the vibraphone. Similar substitutions occur in the crotales, which create a second melodic line that is derived entirely from the original perpetual motion material. By the end of the movement, the single melodic line has been re-orchestrated in to melody and accompaniment.

Son of (—) is about rhythm. Intentionally disjunct, a large part of the challenge of the movement—aside from the inherent complexity of the rhythmic counterpoint—is in maintaining a convincing musical line through its many sections. This frustration is built into the form, starting very strict, but ending with a cathartic burst of near-improvisation.

The third and final Sam, *Wicked Uncle (—)*, asks the performer to navigate a complex musical field in which each mallet of a four-mallet configuration—plus the feet—was conceived as a relatively independent voice. It is as if the performer now has more active limbs than most mere mortals, spread almost too thin.

Three Sams was premiered by Samuel Z. Solomon on May 6th, 2007 at Boston Conservatory's Seully Hall. It lasts approximately 13 minutes, and it dedicated to Sam with endless respect and gratitude.

David T. Little
September 11, 2008

STAGE SETUP

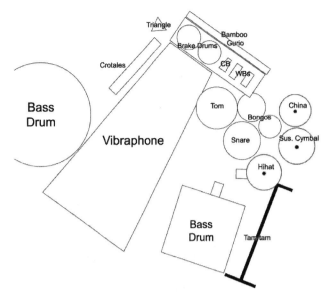

Diagram courtesy of Sam Solomon

PERCUSSION KEY

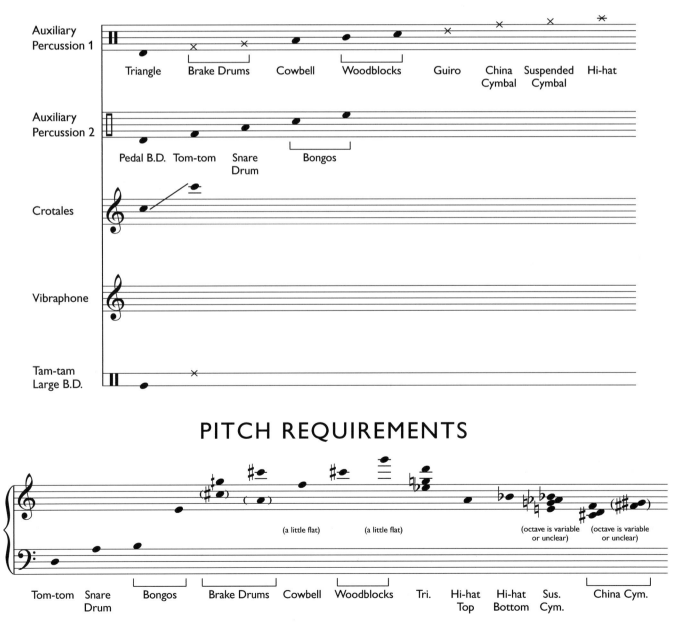

PITCH REQUIREMENTS

(Note: These are the pitches of the instruments for which *Three Sams* was originally composed, and which are largely exploited in the first movement. Please make your best attempt to find instruments as close to these pitches as possible.)

for Sam Z. Solomon

THREE SAMS

DAVID T. LITTLE

(2007)

I. (---)-I-Am

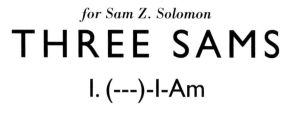

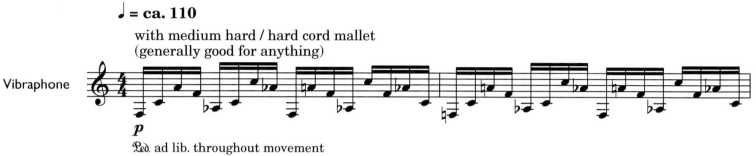

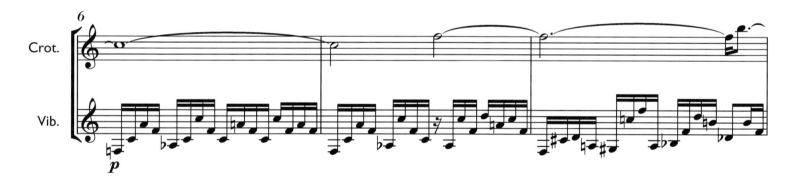

979-0-051-09825-5

February 2018

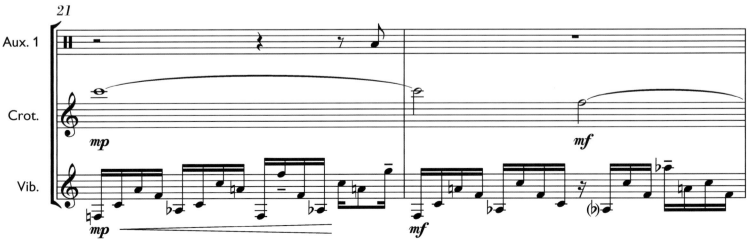

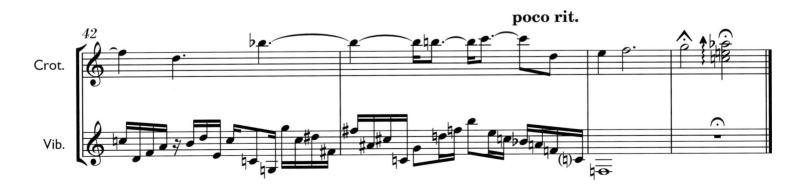

II. Son of (---)

Menacing, ♩ = ca. 120

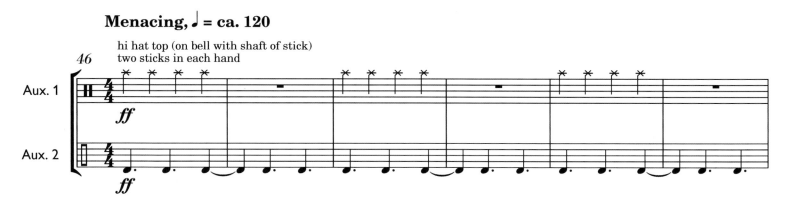

6

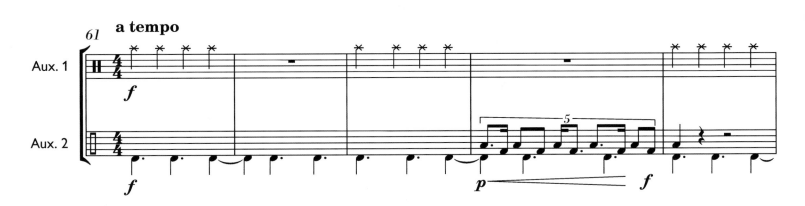

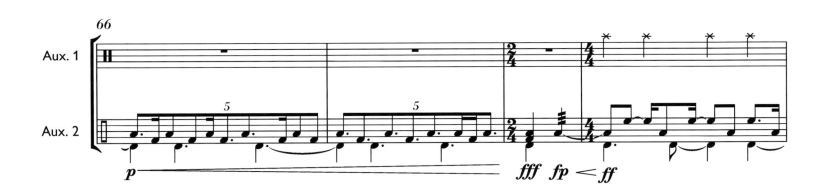

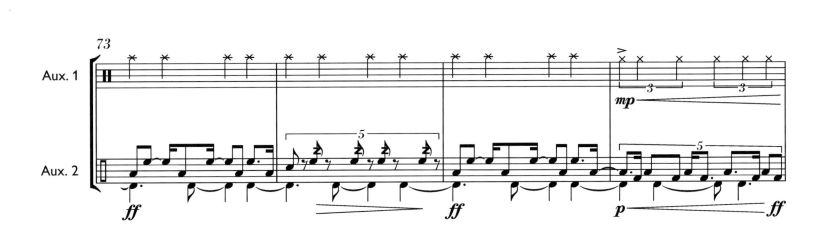

poco rit.

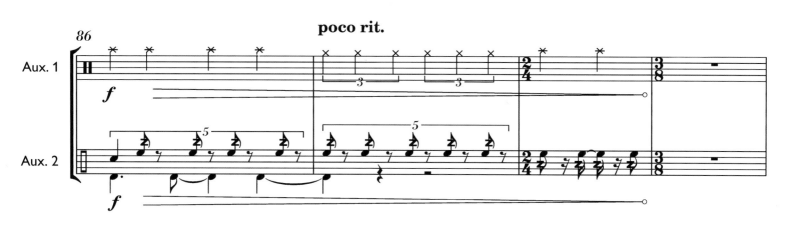

8

A little slower, ♩ = ca. 114

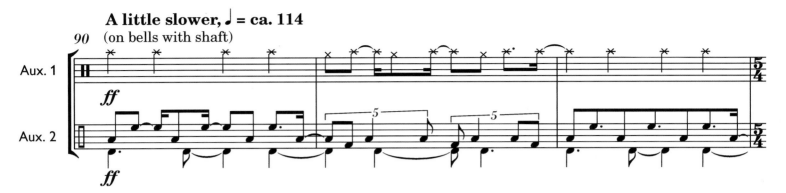

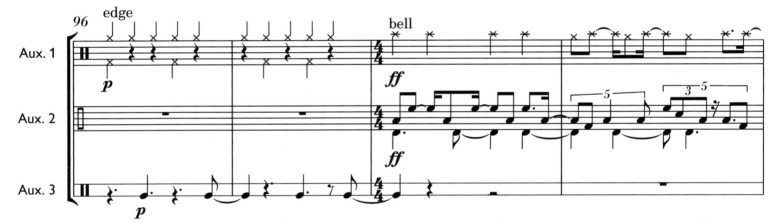

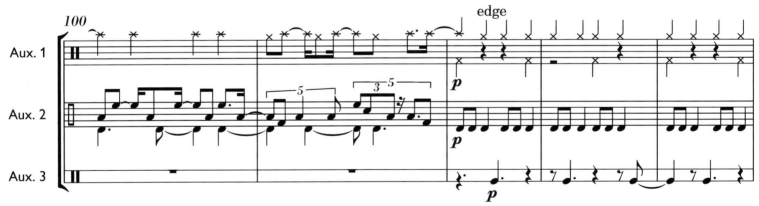

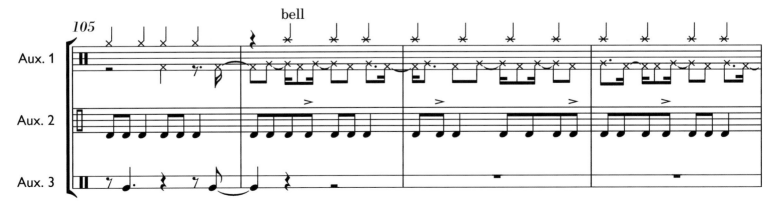

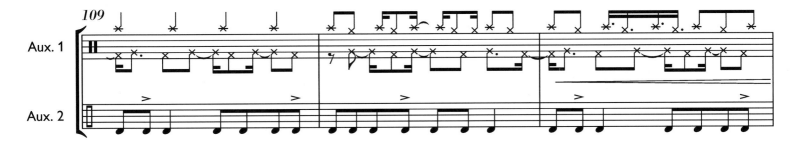

**Freely,
like a dog growling, then barking** *

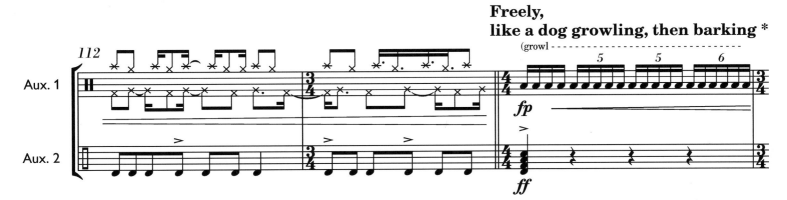

* The theatrically inclined should feel free to vocally growl and bark, imitating this phrase, while they play

Freely, like a dog growling, then barking *

♩ = ca. 100

(approximation of a metered roll)

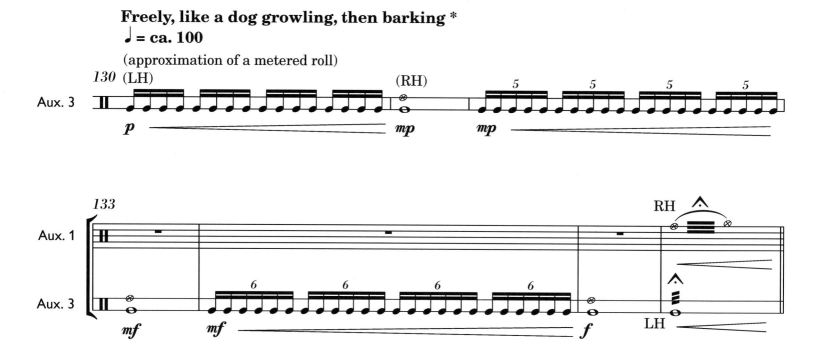

Straight-Jacket Dance Party

♩ = 120 - 132

* As before, feel free to vocalize.

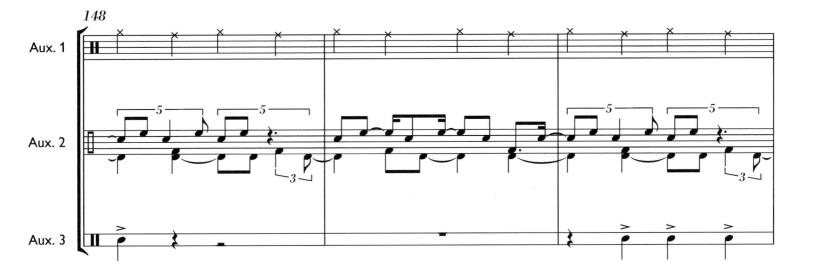

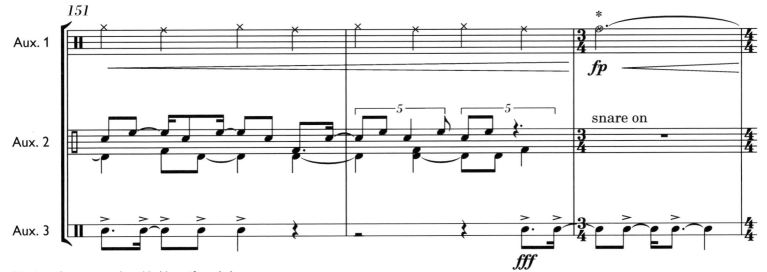

* A <u>short</u> fermata may be added here if needed.

poco accel. to m. 159

with shaft

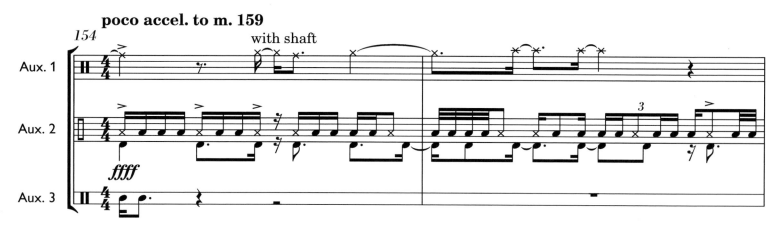

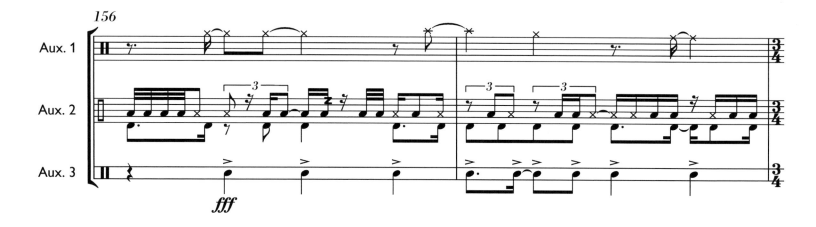

Losing it.

poco accel.

Gradually loosen grip on sticks while continuing to play the written part.
Allow accuracy of part to gradually diminish into chaos.

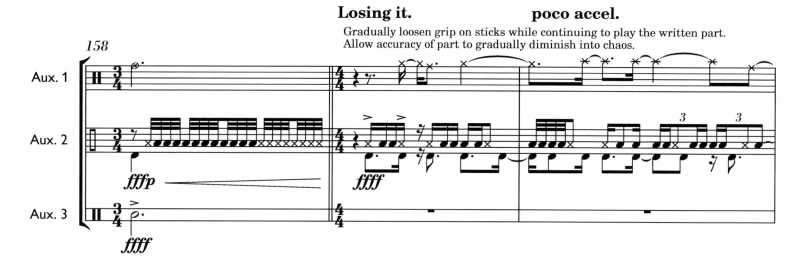

Falling Apart.

Regaining Control Briefly
molto accel.

Wearing Yourself Out.

Totally Falling Apart.

molto rit.

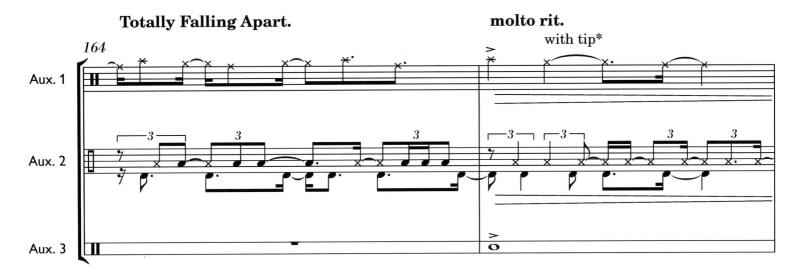

What a Mess.

Cadential

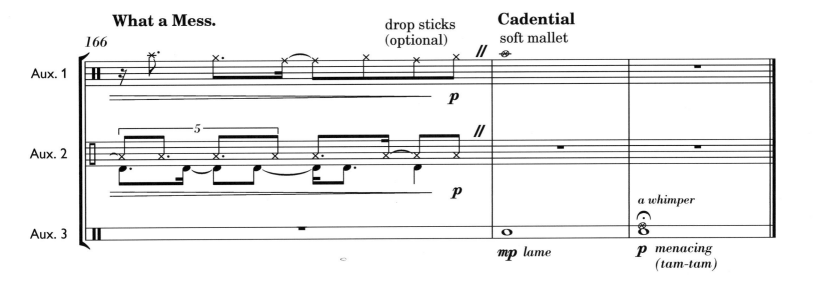

* Also change 'rimshot' to 'rimclick.'

III. Wicked Uncle (---)

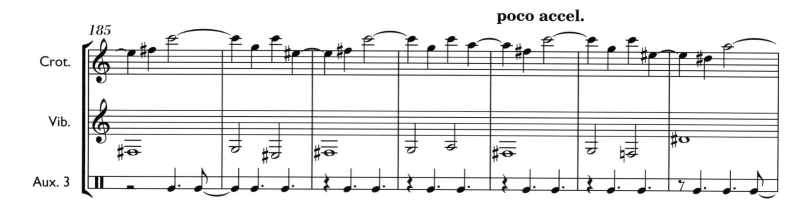

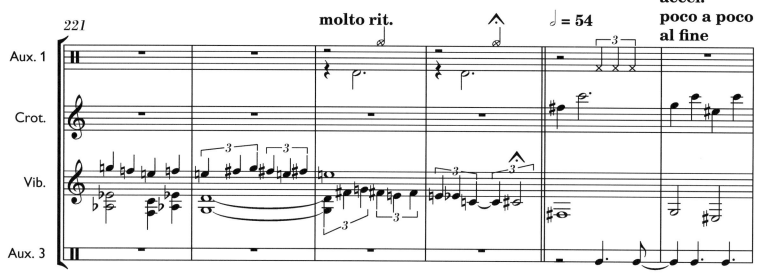

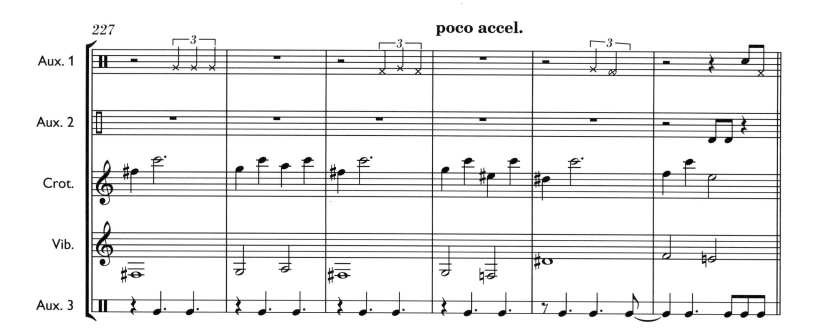

molto rit.

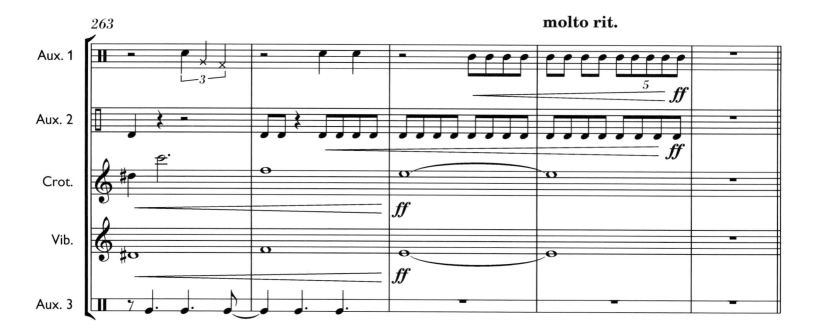

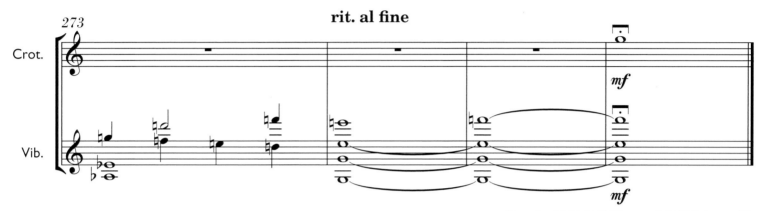

December 20-24, 2006 / January 5, 2007, Princeton NJ
Revised September 2-4, 2007, Weehawken, NJ